RETRO RADIO

SIX DECADES OF DESIGN 1920s–1970s

Mike Tauber

Foreword by Ron Simon

Schiffer Publishing Ltd

4880 Lower Valley Road • Atglen, PA 19310

For Pamela, Wyatt & Rohwan

Other Schiffer Books on Related Subjects
Deco Radio: The Most Beautiful Radios Ever Made by Peter Sheridan. ISBN 978-0-7643-4605-7
The Early Zenith Radios: The Battery Powered Table Sets 1922–1927 by Gilbert M. Hedge with Durell M. Roth. ISBN 978-0-7643-4674-3
Design Chronicles: Significant Mass-Produced Designs of the 20th Century by Carroll Gantz, FIDSA. ISBN 0-7643-2223-0

Cover and Interiors designed by John Cheek
Type set in Market Deco/Century Gothic

ISBN: 978-0-7643-4679-8
Printed in China

Published by Schiffer Publishing, Ltd.
4880 Lower Valley Road
Atglen, PA 19310
Phone: (610) 593-1777; Fax: (610) 593-2002
E-mail: Info@schifferbooks.com

For our complete selection of fine books on this and related subjects, please visit our website at www.schifferbooks.com. You may also write for a free catalog.

This book may be purchased from the publisher. Please try your bookstore first.

We are always looking for people to write books on new and related subjects. If you have an idea for a book, please contact us at proposals@schifferbooks.com.

Schiffer Publishing's titles are available at special discounts for bulk purchases for sales promotions or premiums. Special editions, including personalized covers, corporate imprints, and excerpts can be created in large quantities for special needs. For more information, contact the publisher.

FOREWORD
by Ron Simon

Radio's revolutionary impact on American society is largely forgotten today. Beginning in the early part of the twentieth century, this audio technology disrupted traditional patterns of communication, bringing one live voice into potential contact with a national audience. With the formation of the first commercial network in 1926, the wireless medium helped to foster a national culture and conversation with entertainment and news programs broadcast into millions of homes simultaneously. This mystique and power of analog radio is so difficult to conjure up in this digital century. The programs, which engaged a nation, were much closer in spirit to Victorian entertainment than to the YouTube sensibility. Ironically though, Mike Tauber's photos of retro radios speak volumes to the imagination and possibilities of the medium's golden age.

Legendary humorist Fred Allen once dismissed radio as furniture that talks. But seeing Tauber's pictures, you receive a fine appreciation for that often-exquisite furniture, which is indeed more artistic and sophisticated than most media histories have indicated. In fact, each set uniquely captures the spirit of its times. One can almost hear the calm but authoritative voice of Franklin D. Roosevelt emanating from the rugged, wooden General Electric set of the late Depression era. On the other hand, the stylish 1956 Zenith set with expressive clock and tuner is ready-made for the new sounds of Elvis. I hope that many of these radios become as iconic as the deco Predicta TV set, featuring a bare electronic tube, which has symbolized the pleasure of watching television in the late fifties. Radio may have traveled mysteriously through the air, but it arrived through a very tangible receiver, which deserves our attention.

Radio was always about communication to the single listener in his or her home. The master broadcasters made each member of the audience think that they were speaking directly to them. Much has been written on how radio was processed in the theater of the individual's imagination; each listener created his or her mind picture. But Mike Tauber reminds us that there was another factor in this aural equation. Each listener heard a program through his or her own set, which often framed these voices in the mind's eye. These gorgeous sets have their own stories to tell, while also speaking to the aspirations and the amusements of the radio age. You should definitely listen to Tauber's photographs. They have a lot to say about the radio experience.

Ron Simon is curator of radio and television at the Paley Center for Media and was a contributor to the *Encyclopedia of Radio*.

PREFACE
by Mike Tauber

There was a time when a radio was just a radio, before computers and the Internet, before satellite radio and smart phones. Before television and MTV, the radio was the center of the home, a way for the family to gather to hear the news or listen to music. During one period, the radio was a piece of handcrafted wood furniture, and the limited number of stations available fell silent during part of the day. Now it is possible for us to access movies, music, videos, news media, books and each other through a single, sleek handheld device in our pocket.

The impetus for this project came about when I saw a large collection of vintage radios and was blown away by the diversity in design and materials used to make them over the decades of the twentieth century. As someone born in the early 1970s, I had never seen most of them and thought that many other people probably hadn't either. As a photographer I was inspired to capture each one and present them simply as objects side by side in progression over the decades.

I sourced the radios from private collectors and enthusiasts. I gravitated toward the radios I found interesting and had access to, so this is by no means a comprehensive collection of all the radios ever produced during those six decades. While I have made every attempt to caption each radio with the year it was released, I may be off by a year or two. And for the few where I was unable to find an exact year, I simply captioned it with the decade it was released. My goal for this project was more about the progression of the designs and aesthetics of the devices, hence I am only including the dates as captions and nothing more about the details of each machine and manufacturer.

Retro Radio takes us on a visual journey through the radio's history, encouraging us to consider how far we have come with regard to the marriage of technology and design. The images reveal the diversity of materials, textures, colors, shapes and sizes of a device that only transmitted radio waves and that few people see anymore and perhaps hardly know existed.

THE RADIOS

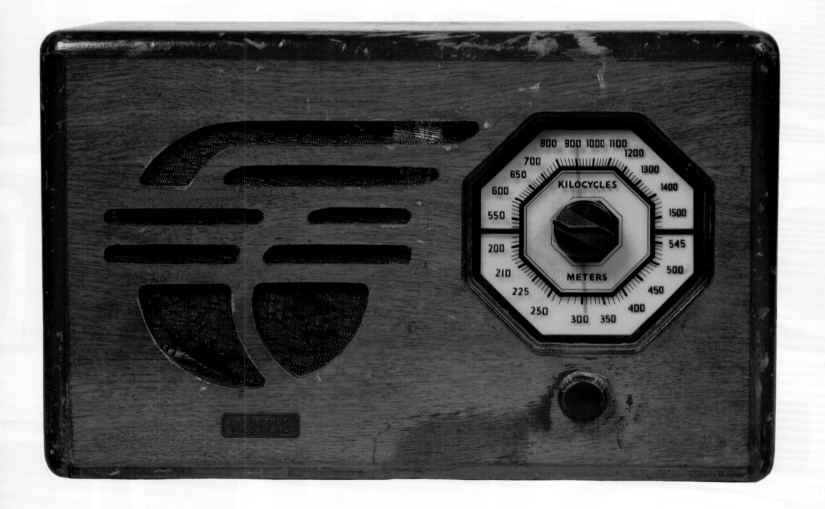

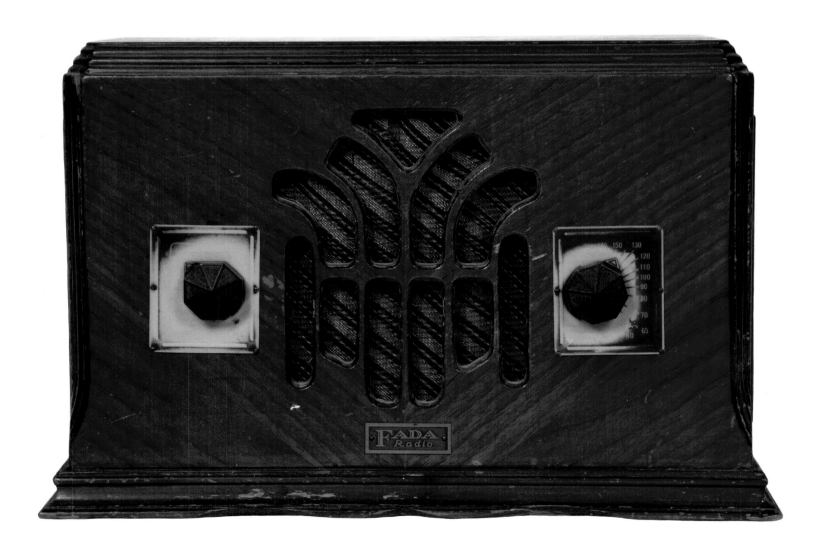

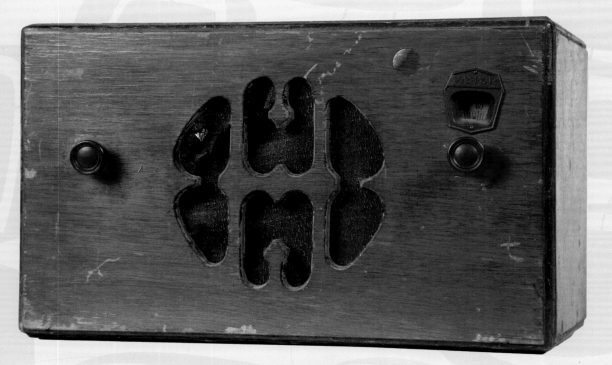

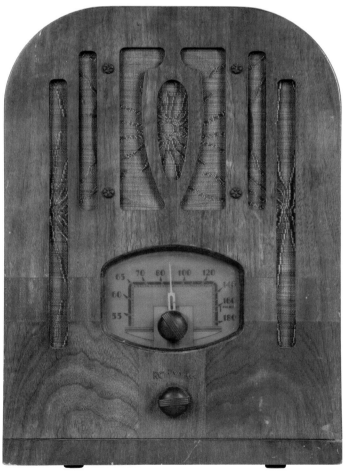

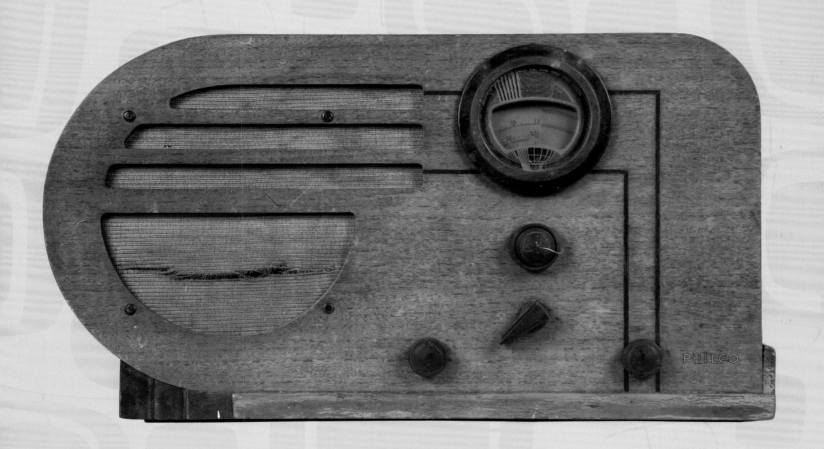

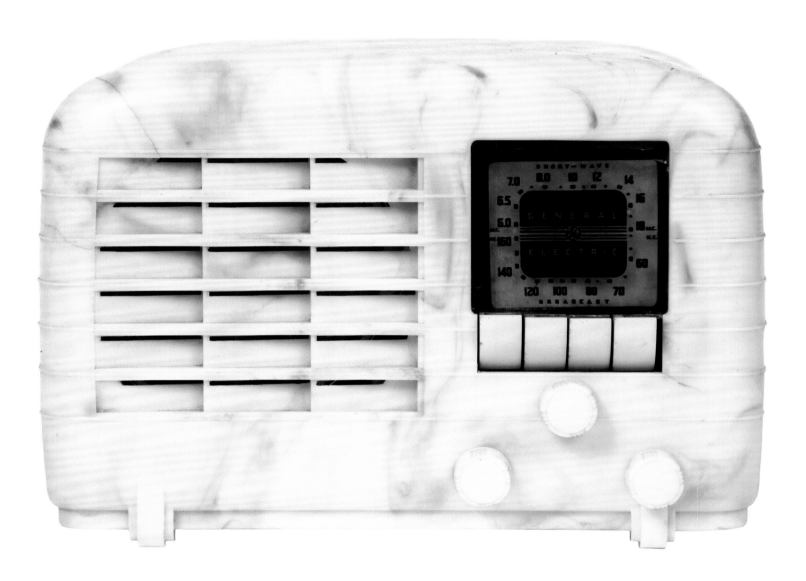

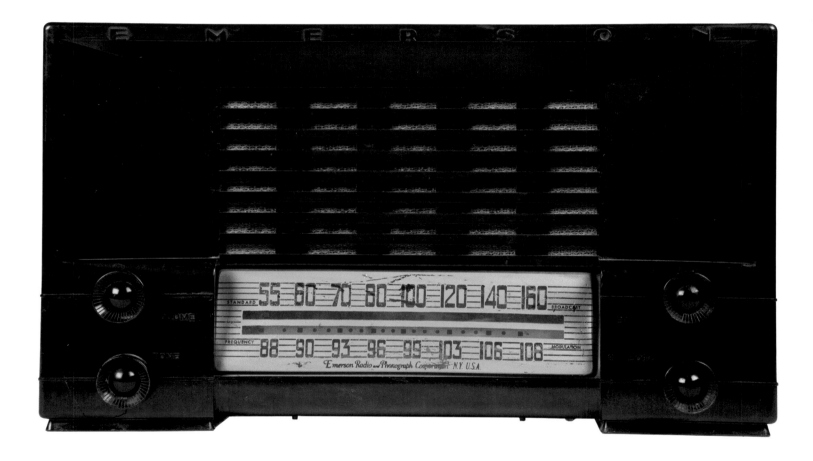

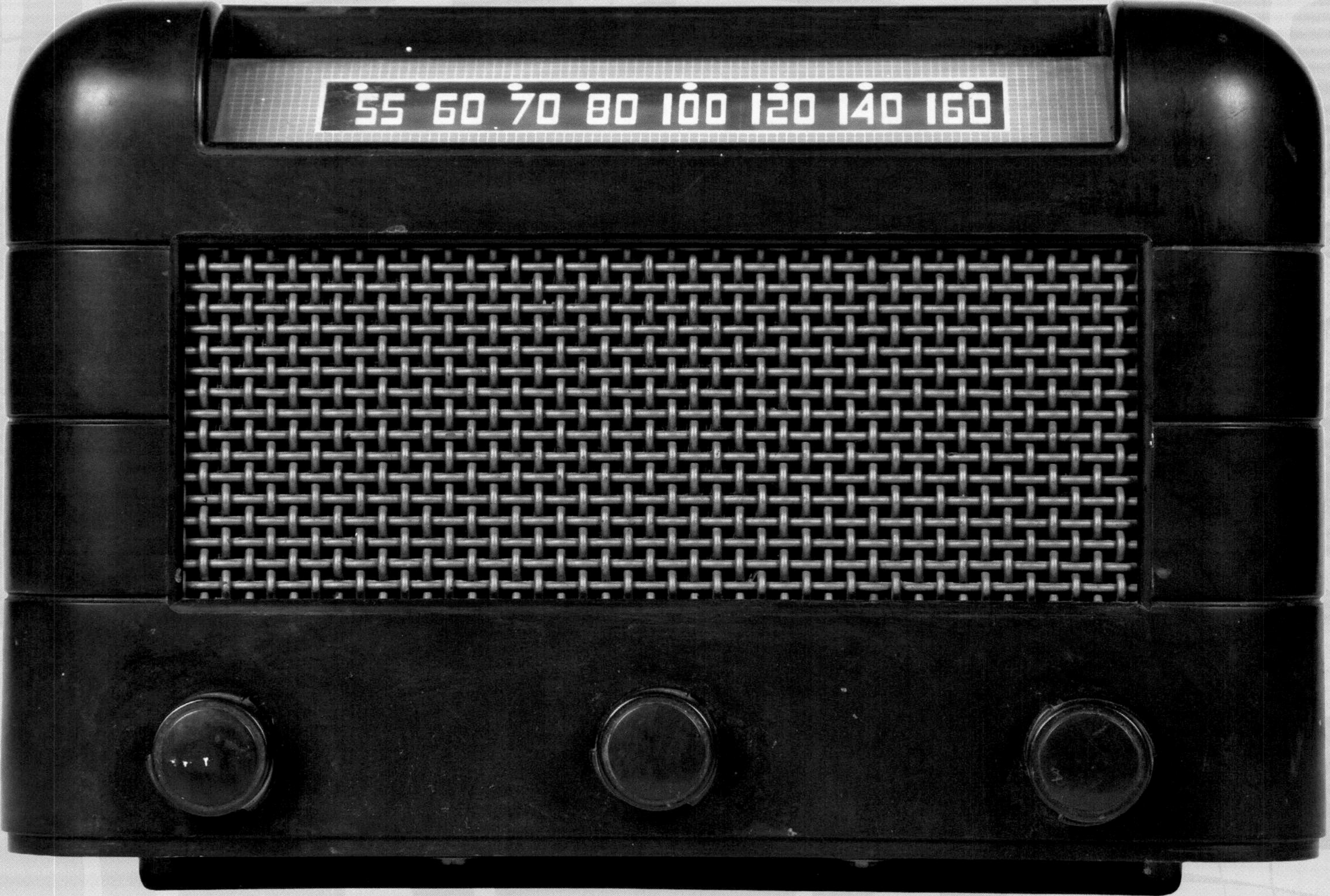
55 60 70 80 100 120 140 160

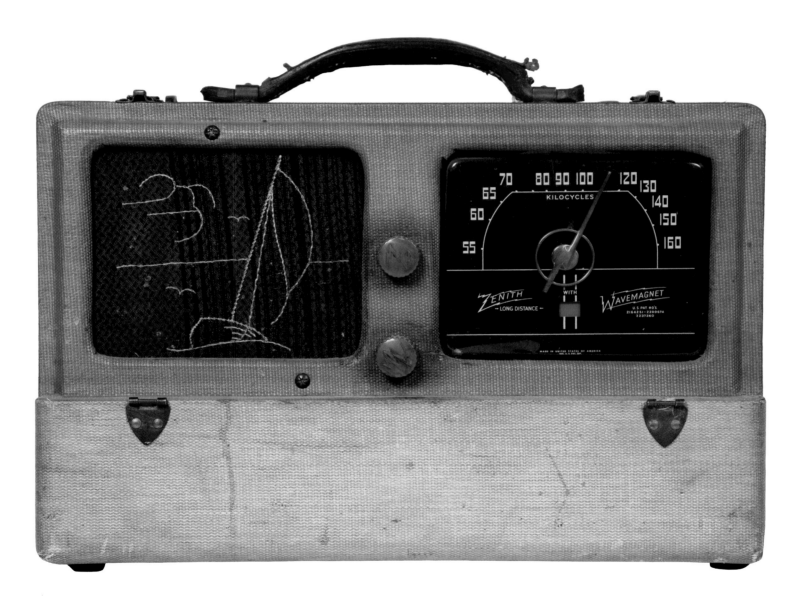

GENERAL ☿ ELECTRIC

55 60 70 80 90 110 130 150 170

PHILCO

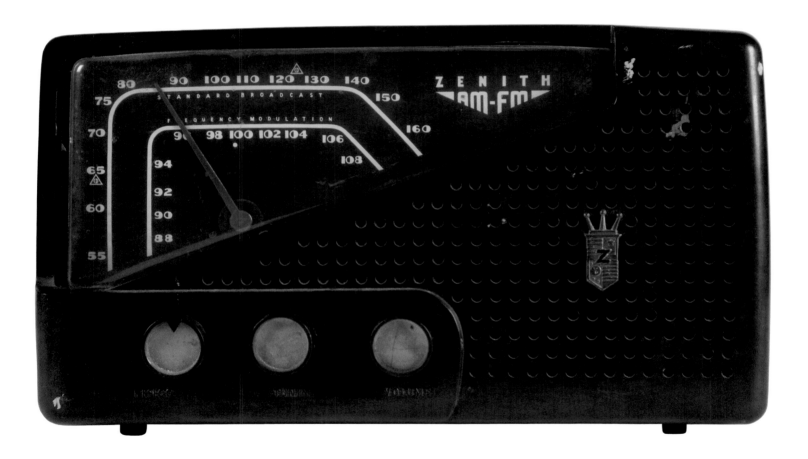

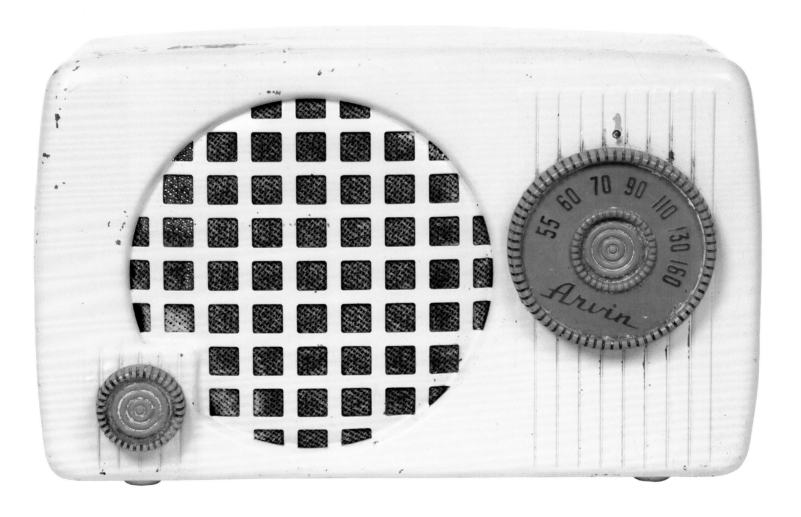

CROSLEY

14   18   24   30   38   48   62   82

ULTRA HIGH FREQUENCY TELEVISION CHANNELS

UHF   VHF   OFF   TUNING

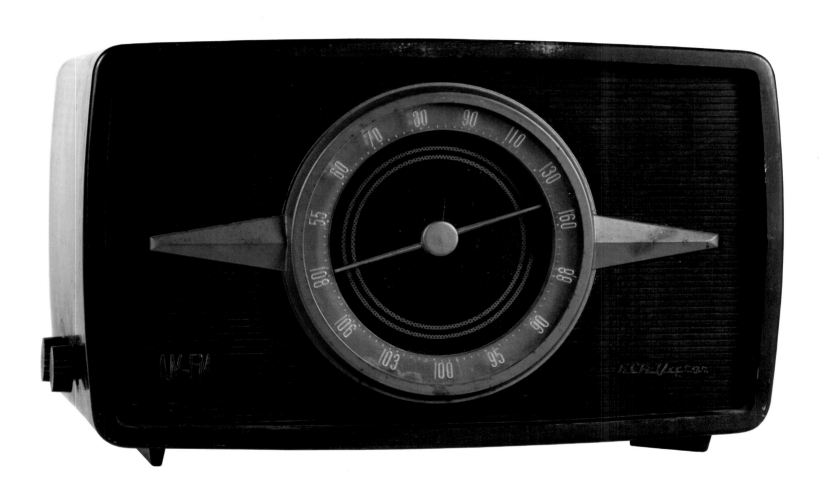

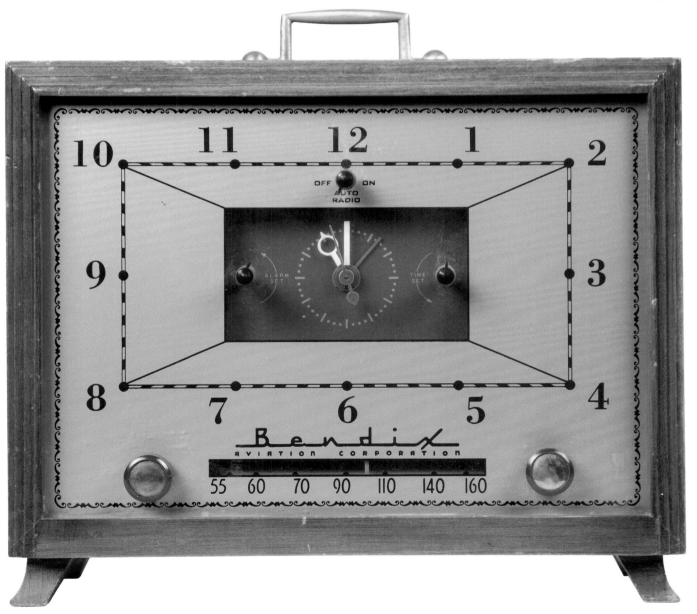

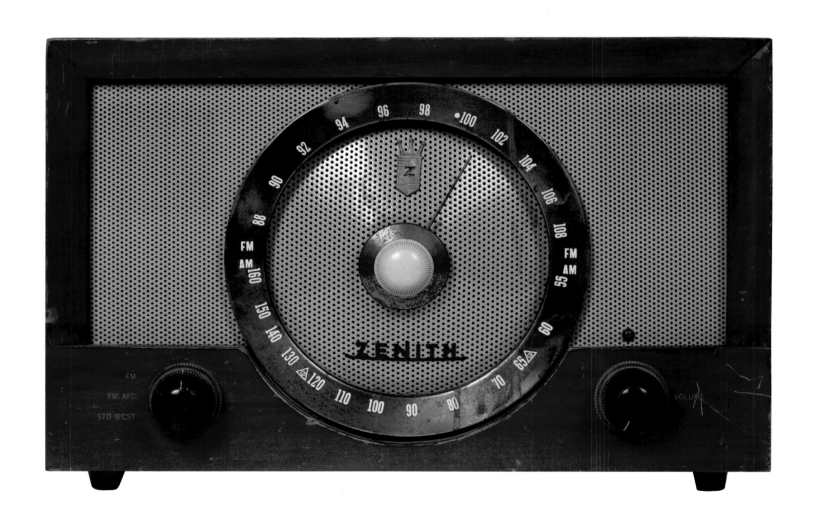

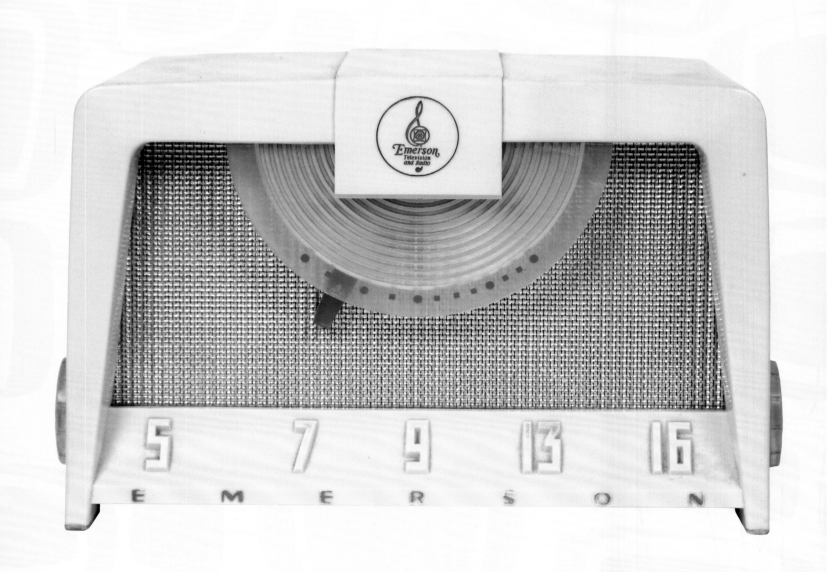

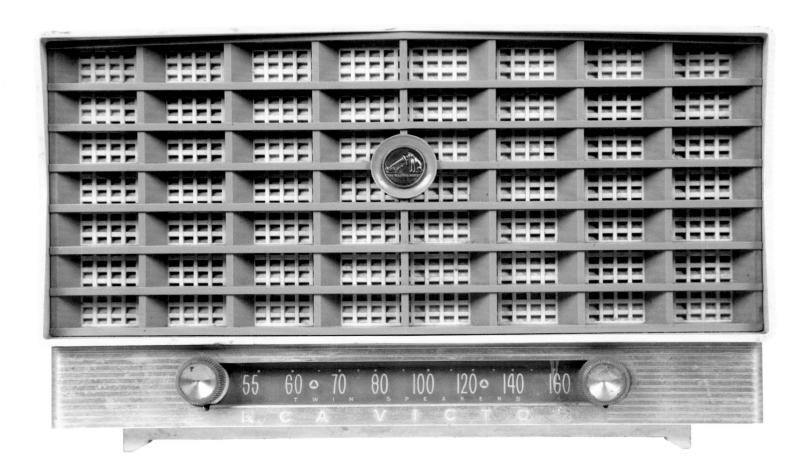

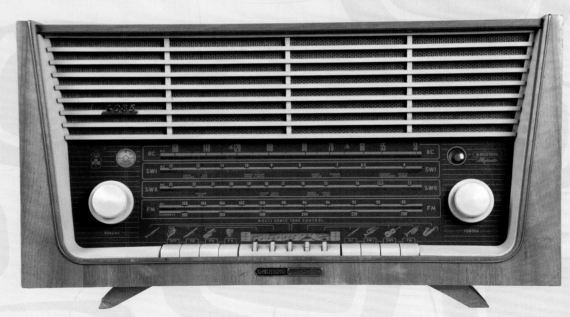

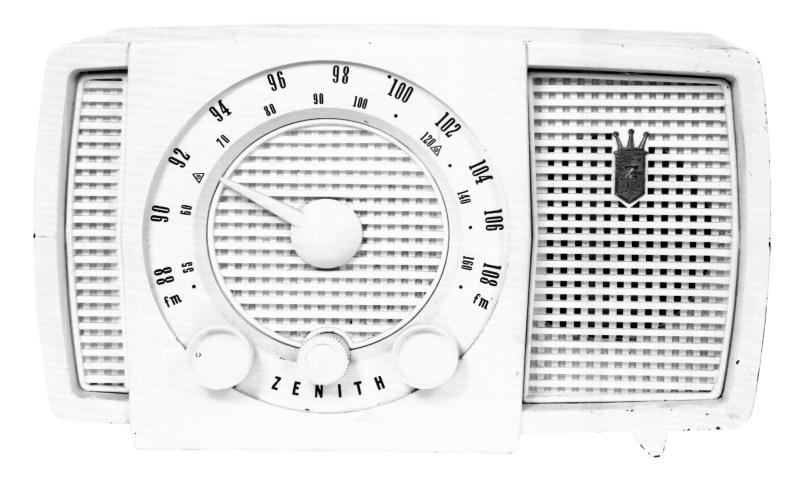

ZENITH
Filter-tenna

VOL. ON-OFF   TONE   TUNING

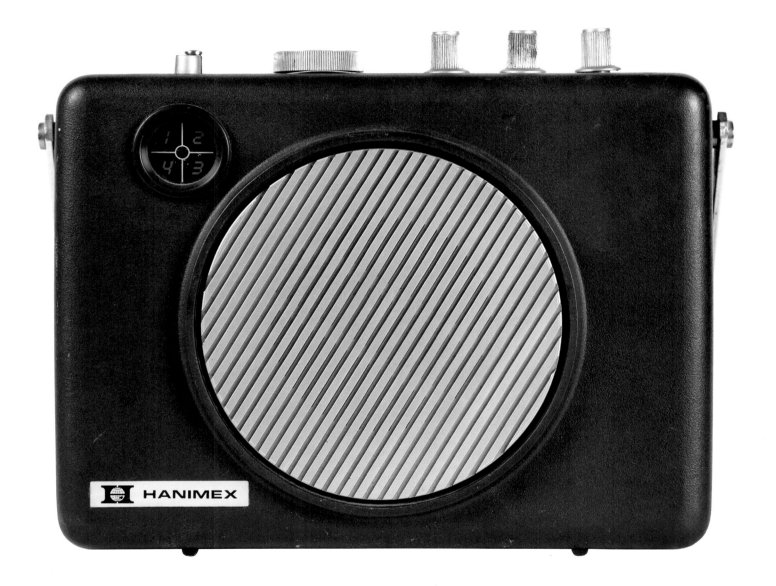

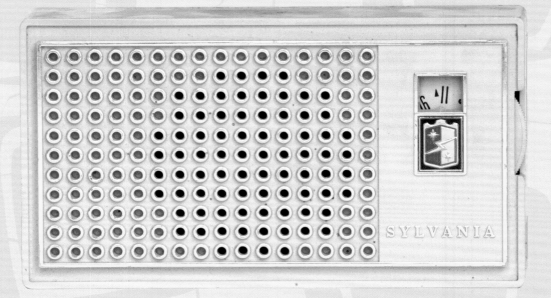

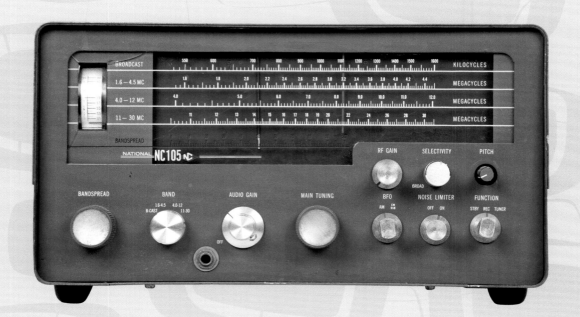

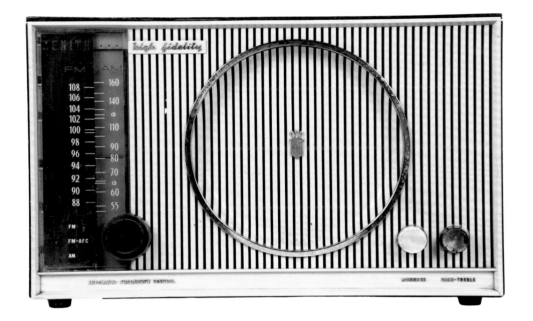

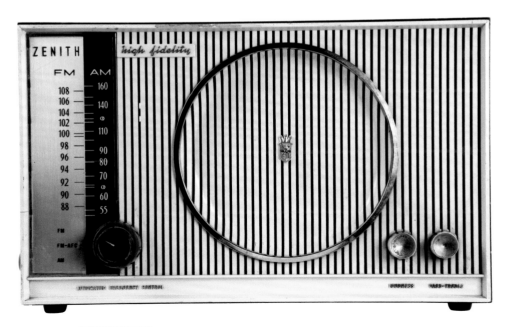

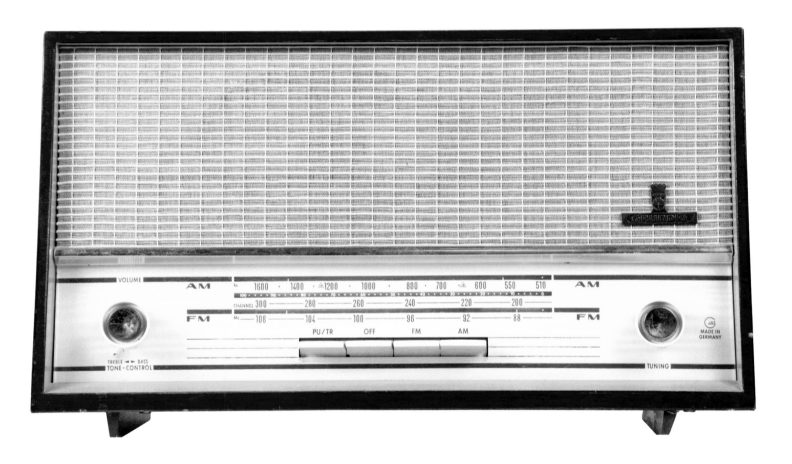

1936 | p. 19

1937 | p. 20

1937 | p. 21

1937 | p. 22

1938 | p. 23

1938 | p. 24

1938 | p. 25

1938 | p. 26

1938 | p. 27

1939 | p. 28

1939 | p. 29

1939 | p. 30

1939 | p. 31

1939 | p. 32

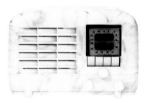

1939 | p. 33

THE 1940s

1940s | p. 34

1940s | p. 35

1940s | p. 36

1940s | p. 37

1940s | p. 38

1940s | p. 39

1940 | p. 40

1940 | p. 41

1940 | p. 42

1940 | p. 43

1940 | p. 44

1941 | p. 45

1941 | p. 46

1941 | p. 47

1941 | p. 48

1942 | p. 49

1946 | p. 50

1946 | p. 51

1946 | p. 52

1946 | p. 53

1946 | p. 54

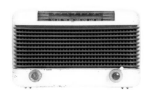
1946 | p. 55

1946 | p. 56

1946 | p. 57

1946 | p. 58

1946 | p. 59

1946 | p. 60

1946 | p. 61

1946 | p. 62

1946 | p. 63

1947 | p. 64

1947 | p. 65

1947 | p. 66

1947 | p. 67

1947 | p. 68

1947 | p. 69

1947 | p. 70

1947 | p. 71

1948 | p. 72

1948 | p. 72

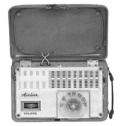

1948 | p. 73

1948 | p. 74

1948 | p. 75

1948 | p. 76

1948 | p. 77

1948 | p. 78

1948 | p. 79

1948 | p. 80

1948 | p. 81

1949 | p. 82

1949 | p. 83

1949 | p. 84

1949 | p. 85

1949 | p. 86

1949 | p. 87

1949 | p. 88

1949 | p. 89

THE 1950s

1950s | p. 90

1950s | p. 90

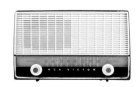
1950s | p. 91

1950s | p. 92

1950s | p. 93

1950s | p. 94

1950s | p. 95

1950 | p. 96

1950 | p. 97

1950 | p. 98

1950 | p. 99

1951 | p. 100

1951 | p. 101

1951 | p. 102

1951 | p. 103

1951 | p. 103

1951 | p. 104

1951 | p. 104

1951 | p. 105

1951 | p. 106

1951 | p. 107

1951 | p. 108

1951 | p. 109

1952 | p. 110

1952 | p. 111

1952 | p. 112

1952 | p. 113

1953 | p. 114

1953 | p. 115

1953 | p. 116

1953 | p. 117

1953 | p. 118

1953 | p. 119

1953 | p. 120

1953 | p. 121

1954 | p. 121

1954 | p. 122

1954 | p. 123

1955 | p. 124

1955 | p. 125

1955 | p. 126

1955 | p. 127

1955 | p. 128

1955 | p. 129

1955 | p. 130

1956 | p. 131

1956 | p. 131

1956 | p. 132

1956 | p. 133

1956 | p. 134

1956 | p. 135

1956 | p. 135

1956 | p. 136

1956 | p. 137

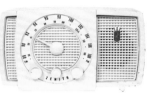
1956 | p. 138

1956 | p. 139

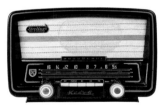
1957 | p. 140

1957 | p. 141

1957 | p. 142

1957 | p. 143

1957 | p. 144

1957 | p. 145

1958 | p. 146

1958 | p. 147

1958 | p. 147

1958 | p. 148

1959 | p. 149

1959 | p. 150

1959 | p. 150

1950s | p. 151

 THE 1960s

1960s | p. 152

1960s | p. 153

1960 | p. 153

1960 | p. 154

1961 | p. 154

1962 | p. 155

1962 | p. 156

1962 | p. 156

1963 | p. 157

1963 | p. 158

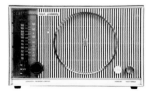
1964 | p. 159

1964 | p. 159

1965 | p. 160

1965 | p. 161

1965 | p. 162

1967 | p. 163

THE 1970s

1970s | p. 164

1972 | p. 165

ACKNOWLEDGMENTS

I would like to thank Dick Demenus whose collection inspired this project and makes up most of this book. Dick was incredibly supportive and helpful and I am grateful. If you find yourself in Manhattan, stop by his store, Tekserve, to see some of his collection on the walls. Thanks to Adam Tyson for his late-night assistance while photographing in Tekserve after hours. I'd like to thank the following people for their feedback, guidance or other assistance: Natalie Kaczinski, Elizabeth Avedon, Frank Meo, and Jamie Cooper.

Thanks to my father Jeff and sister Deb for their support. Finally I would like to thank my beautiful wife Pamela and my two young boys Wyatt and Rohwan for their love, energy and inspiration.

ABOUT THE AUTHOR

Mike Tauber specializes in portraiture, travel, interiors, and architectural imagery. As a Manhattan-based independent photographer, he shoots for both magazines and commercial clients. His work has been featured on NBC's *Today Show*, NPR's *Weekend Edition*, *The Tavis Smiley Show*, as well as other TV, blog, print, and radio outlets across the country. His work has won an International Photography Award, a Young Voices Foundation Award, and has been recognized in the Photo District News Photo Annual. He is the photographer and co-author of the award-winning book *Blended Nation: Portraits and Interviews of Mixed-Race America* (Channel Photographics, 2009), which explores the concept of race in America through the prism of the personal experiences of people of mixed-race heritage.

To view more of Mike's work:
    miketauber.com
    miketauberphoto.com